101 Stupid Things Supervisors Do To Sabotage Success

Peter R. Garber

Mark S. Loper

Richard Chang Associates, Inc.
Publications Division
Irvine, California

101 Stupid Things Supervisors Do To Sabotage Success

Peter R. Garber
Mark S. Loper

Library of Congress Catalog Card Number
97-65523

ISBN   1-883553-94-6

Editors:	Bill Foster and Marcia Robertson
Reviewer:	Shirley Codrey and Karen Johnson
Graphic Layout:	Christina Slater
Cover Design:	Christina Slater and Eric Strand

Richard Chang Associates, Inc.
Publications Division
15265 Alton Parkway, Suite 300
Irvine, CA 92618
(800) 756-8096   (714) 727-7477
Fax (714) 727-7007
E-Mail: info@rca4results.com

About The Authors

Peter R. Garber is Manager of Teamwork Development for PPG Industries, Inc., Pittsburgh, PA. In his work, Mr. Garber deals extensively with supervisors on all levels of the organization helping them develop the skills necessary to meet the many challenges of today's workplace. He is also the author of a number of other management development books.

Mark S. Loper is a freelance writer who specializes in humor. He's written advertising copy, TV and film scripts, a newspaper column, corporate comedy, and has created a program teaching children how to develop their creative writing skills. He's also employed in the corporate marketplace, which he continues to find rich with comic material. On the job and at home, Mark is heavily supervised.

Acknowledgments

This book would not have been possible without "stupid" and useful input from family, friends, and colleagues. Thanks go out to June Loper, Greg Deist, Bill Foster, Holly Hart, Denise Jeffrey, Ruth Stingley, Rich Baisner, Pamela Wade, and Gayle Williams.

Table of Contents

9. Meetings & Other Stupid Stuff 111

Summary 125

Introduction

"There are three great mysteries in life: air to the bird, water to the fish, and human being to himself."

Chinese proverb

Call them managers, executives, supervisors, or just plain bosses. Yet, unknowingly, supervisors often do things that actually decrease the motivation and effectiveness of the people who work for them.

Even the most successful supervisors can relate war stories of stressful employee interactions that occurred while they were growing and developing their skills. But, are we condemned to make the same *stupid* mistakes, often without realizing it? Is it necessary that we learn the hard way, one blunder at a time?

Next Time

As you're leading your team, this book will help you focus on successful strategies. It's a reference tool designed for browsing, and for enjoying.

This book is also useful for new supervisors. And, it's a practical gift for the most experienced supervisors.

Outstanding supervisors work hard to improve their skills and this book will make your progress easier. Now you can avoid making those *stupid* mistakes that make your lives so much more difficult. And you can have fun doing it.

We feel it's far easier to learn when you can also laugh.

So, let *101 Stupid Things Supervisors Do To Sabotage Success* help you better appreciate what is most important to the people who work for you. Help them achieve their potential and while you're doing it, you can achieve your own.

Chapter 1

Communication

#1 What Open Door Policy?

You tell your staff that you're always available and your door's open. Except it's always closed.

What's Wrong?

- You've lied, and it's not just a little white one.

- You've undermined your credibility.

- You're closing an avenue of communication.

- Your lack of accessibility may force your staff to make uninformed, incorrect decisions.

- Everyone's creativity will be diverted because they'll be imagining what you're really doing behind that door.

Some Success Strategies:

If you promise an open door, then open your door. Of course, there will be times when the door closes, but this is to be expected. You want to nurture open communication with your staff and encourage them to come see you with their concerns and/or solutions. Schedule one-on-one meetings with your team members on a regular, ongoing basis to ensure continuous communication.

#2 Does Anybody Really Care?

You ask one of your staff how his weekend was and you listen for a second. But before he can even finish telling you, you're walking away. You do this regularly.

What's Wrong?

- You obviously don't really care how his weekend was.

- This person will resent you for even asking.

- Your reputation for being self-centered and unsympathetic will quickly spread.

- It's rude.

- Nobody will care about your life either.

- You may want to have your hearing checked.

Some Success Strategies:

If, after asking how a person's weekend was, and a lengthy monologue ensues, ask to excuse yourself due to some urgent (imaginary?) matter. It's important to, at least, acknowledge that you're listening. If you don't care, then it's better not to ask. Don't place yourself in a position that can be misinterpreted.

#3 Say It In One Syllable Or Less

You've been practicing your expanding vocabulary in presentations and in memos to your people.

What's Wrong?

✖ You're perceived as pretentious (that's a show-off, but you knew that).

✖ You could use words incorrectly, and your competence would be suspect.

✖ You'll confuse your staff, and if they're confused, their work could suffer.

✖ Who are you trying to impress?

✖ You're not playing Scrabble here.

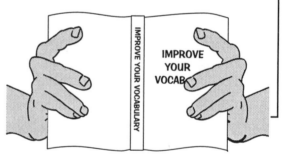

Some Success Strategies:

Talking "up" to your audience can be as bad as talking "down" to them. Speak so your people can understand you. There is certainly nothing wrong with improving your vocabulary, but practicing before the right audience is most important. You'd like to relate to your staff, not alienate them.

#4 I'm Not Mr. Wizard

You're spending too much of your time answering questions about personal leave, vacation requests, overtime pay, etc.

What's Wrong?

☪★ You're not being productive.

☪★ Your department isn't being productive.

☪★ This information isn't being conveyed by the right departments to your people.

☪★ Perhaps the information being conveyed is too confusing.

☪★ You're ready to take a permanent vacation.

Some Success Strategies:

Some of these questions are to be expected, but not so you experience a decline in productivity. If new policy is issued, be sure it is communicated clearly to the appropriate people! If there seems to be confusion, field questions, consolidate them, and get back to your team members within a reasonable time frame. It's important you show interest in these areas of personal concern.

#5 A Simple "NO" Won't Suffice

One of your people has requested a promotion; and, rather than give it much consideration or thought, you just told him NO, it can't happen this year. You don't offer any further discussion.

What's Wrong?

☒ You don't understand the emotional impact of this kind of rejection.

☒ Your employee will be confused and frustrated.

☒ Your employee might look for a new opportunity.

☒ Well, there goes your shot at the Touchy-Feely Sensitive Supervisor of the Year Award.

Some Success Strategies:

If a promotion isn't called for, then explain to your staff member why he won't be promoted. Career planning should be included in each staff member's performance plan. Let him know what his goals and objectives are for his job, and how you'll assist him in getting there. Also, tell him what he can expect upon reaching his goals. Promotions are significant issues. A curt *no*, without an explanation, can cause severe damage. Help your employee understand what's necessary for advancement.

#6 Faster Than A Speeding Bullet?

Your boss keeps piling on one assignment after another; and you, being the good supervisor, just can't say no. Now you're falling farther and farther behind.

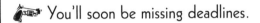

What's Wrong?

- You'll soon be missing deadlines.

- Your boss doesn't realize what you do, what your people do, nor how long these assignments take.

- You're not being open and communicative with your manager.

- Keep it up and you'll soon be leaping off a tall building.

Some Success Strategies:

Explain to your boss that you're facing a backlog. Ask for extensions on earlier deadlines. Ask for more people, resources, or assistance from another department. If this doesn't work, then prioritize your assignments and plan the best you can. Communicate these priorities to your boss and your team members. Keep a log of your rush jobs if you need documentation of why you're falling behind. It might also be time to reveal your true identity as just a mild-mannered supervisor.

#7 Here, I'll Give You My Gold Watch, Just Go Now!

Your boss is retiring soon and doesn't seem to really care about department business anymore. He's in cruise control and won't make decisions. You're ignoring him and sometimes going to his boss on issues that would normally be handled by your direct superior.

What's Wrong?

- Your boss might find out and take offense.

- You're breaking the chain of command when you skip your immediate supervisor.

- You're spending too much of your time running around needlessly.

- Your staff might follow your example and go directly to your boss!

- You just found out your boss is leaving his multimillon dollar estate to his most loyal employees.

© 1993, 1994 AL ROSS

Some Success Strategies:

Sit down with your supervisor and explain your concerns. Let him know how much his mentoring has meant to you. Explain how you'd like that learning to continue until he retires. Offer him another specific challenge. Make his role exciting one more time. Show him how he can still contribute and how his experience is needed. You want to continue developing this partnership, not part on hostile terms.

#8 Show Me The MONEY!

You're never quite sure how to handle the compensation issue, so you basically just tell your staff what they're getting and leave it at that. Even though you're usually strong, it's such an emotional matter that just thinking about it makes you lightheaded and nauseous.

What's Wrong?

- 💰 Your staff needs to understand why they're making what they are, and what their potential is.

- 💰 Ignoring explanations does not make you a better supervisor.

- 💰 You're a weakling.

- 💰 Accepting input from your staff will make setting pay scales more equitable.

- 💰 You may not understand the compensation system either. At the movies, you cry during the previews.

Some Success Strategies:

Open up the discussion on pay with your staff. Be sure they understand the pay plan. When discussing pay (in private, of course), make your employee comfortable. Remember, this is a personal matter. Be prepared with facts and figures. Be forthright with both good and bad news. Also, make only promises that you can keep.

#9 Forget The Annual Report—Let's Hear The Gossip!

There are countless inflammatory rumors, some clinging to truth, some not, circulating in your department. You've taken the position of just ignoring the gossip, and pretending it doesn't exist.

What's Wrong?

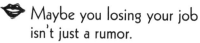 Morale will be affected.

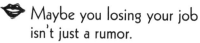 You could lose people acting unwisely due to the rumors.

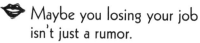 You're "fanning the flames" by not confronting the truth.

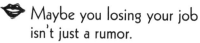 You're losing your credibility.

 Maybe you losing your job isn't just a rumor.

Some Success Strategies:

Confront the rumors and substitute with as many facts as you feel prudent. Correct false information immediately. Be proactive and write memos, a newsletter, or have meetings to maintain open and factual communications.

#10 Do You Read Palms Too?

You think you know the answer before you even hear the question.
This is frustrating your staff, who can't seem to ever make their points or finish their thoughts.

What's Wrong?

- You may not fully understand the problem.

- You may make misinformed decisions that lead everyone on a "wild goose chase."

- You're operating in a "ready-fire-aim" mode.

- Decisions you make could impact the entire organization.

- Your staff will look for another supervisor to work for, one who listens.

- You think you're ready for "Jeopardy."

Some Success Strategies:

Adopt a "look before you leap" attitude about solving problems.
Allow the facts to be discovered before making a decision. Give credit to your people by listening to what they have to offer.

#11 The Bark Is The Bite

You tend to yell. That's just you. When something isn't done right, you yell at your people.

What's Wrong?

- You hurt people's feelings.

- You may say things that you don't really mean.

- You look childish and unprofessional.

- Your people will fear you, but not respect you.

- Your department will be the only one where everyone considers earplugs a necessary accessory.

Some Success Strategies:

Think before you raise your voice. Consider a better way to get your point across to others. Count to ten, maybe a hundred. Take a few deep breaths. Yell at yourself in the confines of a soundproof office or your car. You'll be healthier for it, and so will your staff. If you think yelling and intimidation are proper supervision techniques, you shouldn't be a supervisor.

#12 I'll Get Right Back To You

(Right, And The Check's In The Mail)

You have a tendency not to return calls right away. Particularly *after* you tell people you'll get right back to them. And some of these return calls are important!

What's Wrong?

- ⊠ Unfulfilled expectations make people frustrated and angry.

- ⊠ Others feel you're just putting them off.

- ⊠ You'll damage your reputation.

- ⊠ Your questions, concerns, and calls will go unanswered.

- ⊠ Frankly, my dear, you don't seem to care.

Some Success Strategies:

Try to respond to every inquiry within a reasonable and appropriate time period. If necessary, take notes during the call and determine how long it will take to answer the questions. Make a written note to get back to the caller, don't just store it in your mental inventory. And if you can't get back to the party right away, then tell them that.

#13 Maybe That Ringing Sound Scares Him

You rarely answer the phone and rarely respond to your voice mail. Your staff sees you around the office, they talk to you face-to-face, but you never pick up the phone! You call back when you can find the time.

What's Wrong?

📞 People don't get the information they need, and it could be important!

📞 People will stop trying to call you.

📞 Relationships will be negatively impacted.

📞 Your boss may not appreciate your non-responsiveness.

📞 It'll be terrible when you're replaced by voice mail.

Some Success Strategies:

Don't allow voice mail to be a substitute for you. Answer your phone as much as possible. Update your voice mail as to your whereabouts if you're not around your phone. Let the caller know when you're returning. Give names and numbers of others to contact if you're not available. Consider a pager.

#14 Okay, Who Pulled The Cord In The Back Of His Neck?

You love to hear yourself talk. You know that sometimes you get carried away, but you've got meaningful things to say, a wonderful voice, and singing in the shower just isn't enough!

What's Wrong?

 Others never get a chance to talk.

 You become known as a "know-it-all."

 You miss out on what others have to say.

 People will try to avoid you.

 You probably forgot to wash under your arms.

Blah, Blah, Blah

Some Success Strategies:

Become conscious of the time you spend talking. Practice talking less. Let others be heard. Have someone give you a signal if they feel you've talked long enough. Put together notes on what you want to say and stick to it! Take a course on effective listening techniques.

#15 I'm Not A Sheep

People really like to be aware of what the Big Boss is thinking in your organization. She's the Top Dog, the Big Cheese, the Head Honcho. You don't like to just follow the leader, so you don't do a very good job of conveying her philosophy and direction.

What's Wrong?

- People worry unnecessarily about things that may never happen.

- You lose an opportunity to strengthen the liaison between the top management and your staff.

- The rumors can fly about what was "supposedly said."

- People feel ignored and left out of the "loop."

- People don't have the chance to recognize their role in the "big picture."

Some Success Strategies:

Share what you can with your team members following meetings you have with your boss. Do this in a timely manner. Perhaps the Big Boss can meet with your people occasionally. Encourage your staff to ask relevant questions and express their concerns. This will offer them a look at their organization from a different perspective.

#16 Cloak & Dagger

You're comfortable working with hidden agendas. So you don't like to reveal "everything" to your staff as they take on new assignments. Sometimes they just don't need to know the reasons why. Besides, you might have an ulterior motive.

What's Wrong?

- Your staff is upset because they are being tricked or deceived.

- Your staff is suspicious of being manipulated.

- Assumptions made by unknowing staff can lead to disaster.

- Your credibility is suspect.

- The hidden video camera in your stapler might be overdoing it.

Some Success Strategies:

Openly explain the purpose and objectives of the assignment with everyone. Make the agenda you communicate the agenda you follow. There will be times when your staff cannot be totally informed. Make them aware of this, for it's important to kindle the spirit of shared knowledge and goals.

Chapter 2

Improving Performance

#17 Give Him Space, He Can't Breathe!

You issue an assignment, and to be sure it's being done correctly, you tend to hover over your associate until it's completed.

What's Wrong?

✔ You're not showing confidence in your employee.

✔ It's not a good use of your time unless your employee really needs your help.

✔ Your employee may not perform well under constant scrutiny.

✔ You're creating resentment.

✔ With habitual hovering, your associate could open his refrigerator at home, take out the Swiss cheese, and you'll remind him not to forget the mustard.

© 1992,1994 CHARLES BARSOTTI

Some Success Strategies:

Your follow-up and concern is understandable, but let your associate spread his wings. Casually ask about the assignment when discussing other matters. If it's an important assignment, schedule time to discuss its progress. Remember, you're building a team and this team must be developing their abilities. Give them the opportunity to test these abilities; only you can offer that.

#18 I'll Need It By Yesterday

When assignments are given by you, results are expected in an unreasonable short period of time.

What's Wrong?

🕐 You'll probably get sloppy, inaccurate results.

🕐 It'll be difficult to keep good people.

🕐 The people you do keep will feel you have no idea what their job actually entails.

🕐 Your reputation will suffer (if it improves, then you need more help than this book).

Some Success Strategies:

Ask your employee what period of time may be necessary to complete the assignment. Empathize with her, but if a deadline is mandatory, be sure she recognizes why the deadline is important. Determine if she can meet it. Outline the key criteria so she can remain on track. If a deadline is met with success, reward your employee with positive feedback. She'll probably be more eager to tackle the next job. Be open to renegotiating the deadline or to securing additional support.

#19 And Do The Windows!

Your department always seems to get the "dirty" or unwanted jobs and you can't seem to find a way to avoid them.

What's Wrong?

 Morale of your staff will suffer.

 Your staff will look for work in another department, one that gets respect.

 You may be productive, but so what?

 Your self-respect will take a beating.

 At home, you stop helping with the dishes.

Some Success Strategies:

Remember, you're always working on priority assignments (even if you're not). Be ready to attach significance to the most boring and trivial of projects. This will impress upon others that you simply can't take on their unwanted jobs.

#20 To Err Is Human, But Not When Working For Me

You overreact and reprimand your team severely when they make mistakes. Sometimes their missing deadlines and careless work habits just drives you *crazy!*

What's Wrong?

☞ You need to lighten up!

☞ Staff paralysis from fear will impair productivity.

☞ Perhaps the mistakes are beginning with poor communications from you.

☞ Good people who might like to take a few chances won't want to work for you.

☞ Supervising could be extremely difficult if you're wearing a strait jacket.

Some Success Strategies:

Be tolerant and remember that people grow from mistakes. Clarify all your instructions and be sure all imposed deadlines are reasonable. Be aware that some mistakes are caused by a "breakdown" somewhere else in the process. Maybe, even, from another department.

#21 Goals Without Nets

You think goal setting is overrated. You're more comfortable working without specific goals. Instead, you prefer to deal with what's on your agenda day-to-day and work more reactivity.

What's Wrong?

O You, your manager, and your team will never know where you're going.

O You're neglecting an important role of supervision— leadership.

O If you don't know you're going, any path will take you there.

O You'll work on "important" projects that are not focused on end results or goals.

O Your work habits are better suited for something more menial, like pumping gas.

Some Success Strategies:

Write down your goals and those of your department. Make sure they're SMART goals (Specific, Measurable, Agreed Upon, Realistic, and Time-Bound). Reward those that achieve their goals and penalize those who don't. Have both short-term and long-term goals.

#22 Wow, A Triple Axle— That's A 9.7!

You have a tendency to judge your staff on quick impressions, rather than on their whole body of work. This makes for an easy performance evaluation, but...

What's Wrong?

 That "snapshot" may be inaccurate.

 You're jeopardizing the support of your staff with perfunctory judgments.

 Performance evaluations are very important and aren't intended to be "easy."

 Did you forget these evaluations reflect on you, the supervisor?

 You did the same thing with your last car purchase, and everybody still laughs at your Gremlin.

Some Success Strategies:

Meet with each of your people and agree on performance goals over a set period of time. Keep a detailed record of accomplishments during this period. Discuss ongoing performance with your employee throughout this period. Agree on an evaluation rating. Maintain open communication lines and work on improving deficient skills of your employee. Also, ask employees to share their opinions of you. Uh, oh!

#23 Delegation: The Gift Of Giving (But Not To Yourself)

You've given one of your staff an assignment and somehow, you end up doing the job. This is not what you thought delegation was all about.

What's Wrong?

 You're a victim of reverse delegation.

 Your staff member is not acting responsibly.

 Others in your department could follow suit.

 This interferes with your own list of issues and priorities.

 Simple tasks are being pushed up to higher levels for execution.

 Keep it up and soon you'll have to fire everyone and do all their jobs.

Some Success Strategies:

Encourage your team members to make decisions. If an employee is confused, train him yourself or offer additional training with another departmental employee. Suggest the team concept if the employee is new or inexperienced. Keep yourself out of the picture except for recommendations and suggestions. If asked to help out, limit your involvement to providing adequate levels of support and/or direction as needed, and nothing further. Ensure that the organization priorities are kept in check.

#24 When Time Off Makes You Cry, "Time Out!"

When any one of your people takes time off—vacation, illness, etc.—your department's level of productivity drops perceptibly.

What's Wrong?

♦ Poor planning on your part.

♦ No one knows what the missing person does.

♦ No one has the time to do the missing person's job.

♦ The remaining staff will be under great pressure.

♦ You almost go out of business during flu season.

Some Success Strategies:

Someone should know how to do each task in your department. Prioritize assignments if overloaded. Utilize temps. Offer flexible scheduling. Cross train the employees in your department so they can step in when needed.

#25 And It Gives You Varicose Veins, Too!

You're under intense pressure and it's making you irritable. You're also making silly mistakes, and you're going home with splitting headaches. You tell yourself it's just a little stress, and gulp aspirin.

What's Wrong?

○ You're not able to calm yourself.

○ You're taking on too much.

○ What you're taking on, you're taking too seriously.

○ You're becoming less effective on the job.

○ If you don't have a shift in perspective, things will never get better.

○ You're on the edge of becoming an aspirin "junkie."

Some Success Strategies:

Relax. It's just a job. Change the way you do your job physically. Try standing up instead of sitting down. Try a few isometrics to loosen up your muscles. Do a cartwheel. Carefully. Meditate for a few minutes. Exercise before or after work. Breathe deeply. Visualize a relaxing scene (perhaps a sandy beach). And stay away from caffeine; this may augment your stress levels.

#26 And Then At 10:00 We Have The Earth Exploding

One of your people—an eternal pessimist—can't find anything positive about a project, a goal, or even an achievement. It's always going to rain, you'll never get the assignment finished on time, and he'll never win the lottery. Even if he does buy a ticket.

What's Wrong?

⚜ His negativity will damage the department's confidence.

⚜ No one will want to work with him.

⚜ Any challenging assignment he undertakes will require great effort on his part, and yours.

⚜ He's the perfect Cubs fan.

Some Success Strategies:

Point out the successes the department has achieved. Show how this success is going to continue. Offer him further training if he feels this will help. Build his self-esteem. Pair him with your most positive thinkers, your "can do" people.

#27 From Redhead To Hot Head

One of your best people has a volatile temper. Lately, the job pressures seem to be getting to him; and, though still under control, he seems to be smoldering underneath. He's lost it twice and shouted at his co-workers, and his complexion seems to be shifting to the same permanent, ruddy color as his hair.

What's Wrong?

💣 He could become a distraction to your staff.

💣 He's disrupting the workflow.

💣 The pressure seems to be building within this person.

💣 He's beginning to look like an upside-down thermometer.

Some Success Strategies:

After recognizing his condition, try to channel his anger into constructive tasks. Talk to him and see if he "unloads." Try to isolate the anger. Give him time off. Suggest another conduit for release: exercise, a hobby, maybe a long, cross-country drive (on a bicycle). You need to defuse him. Determine what the root cause is, and make appropriate adjustments.

#28 Maybe A Teensy Weensy Part Was My Fault

You're new on the job and you want everyone to think you're perfect. You just can't bring yourself to admit to making a mistake or doing anything out of the ordinary.

What's Wrong?

☺   You show how insecure you really feel.

☺   You lose credibility.

☺   You'll be afraid to take any risks.

☺   Your people will feel reluctant to admit their mistakes.

☺   Someone else may get blamed for your mistakes.

☺   Now, how do you explain those six missing honey-dipped doughnuts and the sugar on your lips?

Some Success Strategies:

Grow up and be willing to admit your mistakes. Accept the responsibility for making them. Learn from your mistakes (you've probably never heard that one before). Before making a decision, think about its ramifications. Think about what you've done in the past. See if experience can guide you. If assistance is needed, ask those who have the experience. Wipe your mouth.

#29 101 Stupid Questions

Part of your management style is to ask questions. In fact, you're constantly asking questions of your people, perhaps to the point where they resent it.

What's Wrong?

- Your employees feel you're always checking up on them.

- They'll constantly be preparing for your questions, and ignoring their work.

- They'll question your confidence in them.

- They will resent you and eventually, probably loathe you.

- You should be taking the census.

Some Success Strategies:

Ask relevant questions. Don't waste everyone's time asking inane ones. Know what you need, go, and search for it. Your queries should be crafted to the situation. They may be direct or indirect, but be prepared to move on once you're satisfied. Let your people get back to their jobs.

#30 That Earthquake Wasn't My Fault

You're constantly getting blamed for things out of your control. You're the departmental supervisor, and also its scapegoat.

What's Wrong?

☒ Your taking the blame may be unjust.

☒ By placing the blame on you, the true cause of the problem may not be found.

☒ You might, as a scapegoat, begin to believe that you actually are to blame for everything that goes wrong in the organization.

☒ You'll get much less done because you're handling other people's problems.

☒ You're being blamed for the tornado at the last departmental picnic.

Some Success Strategies:

Sit down and talk with your manager about this situation. Give specific examples of where you've been unfairly maligned. Explain what impact this is having on you and your department. Try to follow an accusation back to its source. Do not accept any more blame that is unfair or unjust.

#31 My Coffee's Under There Somewhere

You're the model of disorganization. You've got stacks of papers covering your desk, books all over the floor, and you still can't find that shoe you took off last Tuesday. And where's that urgent memo you wanted to send to your boss?

What's Wrong?

 You have little idea what's going on.

 You waste a tremendous amount of time searching for things.

 You're setting a poor example for your staff.

 Your office is not a conducive place for discussing business.

You're inevitably running late or missing deadlines because you can't find things.

Some Success Strategies:

Take a course, read a book, or listen to a tape on organization. Act on each piece of paper the first time it crosses your desk. File it, read it, or dispose of it. Don't just stack it. Keep a daily list of things you have to do. Prioritize. Develop a simple, but effective filing system. Return calls as soon as possible. Try to minimize interruptions. Buy a shredder. A large one.

#32 Don't Bother Me, Just Keep Up The Good Work

You take your department's efficiency for granted and almost don't even notice who's doing what anymore. The projects, the faces, are all blending together. Everything's running smoothly without you even getting involved.

What's Wrong?

☹ You're bored because you're not involved anymore.

☹ You're not realizing the potential of your people.

☹ Your people feel unappreciated.

☹ You're not recognizing the accomplishments of your staff.

☹ You'll die, and no one will notice.

Some Success Strategies:

Remain part of the action by staying involved. Ask your team members what they would like to achieve. Show them how it can be done. Instill a sense of spirit and excitement by forming teams and rewarding the winners with incentives. Always be developing new challenges. Become part of the team concept and eliminate any worries about complacency.

#33 Bring Out The Ouija Board

Lately, you've been very indecisive. Your resolutions are taking far too long; and, after you make them, you're not even sure they're the right decisions.

What's Wrong?

➢ You're slowing down productivity.

➢ Your second guessing impairs your confidence.

➢ Management won't like what they see.

➢ Your staff will lose confidence in you.

➢ How will you ever pick out the right wallpaper?

Waiting Long?

Some Success Strategies:

Ask other supervisors and managers how they arrive at their decisions. Start a journal analyzing decisions, yours and others. Note who makes the decisions, dedicated to where they got the information, the deadlines, the process, and the results. Collect this data and examine the resulting matrix. Use this matrix to assist you in your decisions. Recognize when snap decisions are appropriate. Be aware of the magnitude of any decision you make.

Chapter 3

Motivation

#34 Promises, Promises

You promised your staff a bonus months ago if they continued to beat deadlines, which they have. Now they're upset because the offered bonuses seem inadequate.

What's Wrong?

○ Mutiny in the making.

○ You may now find yourself missing deadlines.

○ Your promises mean as much as campaign promises.

○ Your credibility has been undermined.

○ It may not even help if you cross your heart and hope to die.

Some Success Strategies:

It's certainly okay to make promises, but be certain your staff knows what's expected from them. And, it's also important to know what they expect from you. Your promises should be specific and fulfilled when agreed-upon goals are achieved. Be sure that the reward "matches" the assignment.

#35 Take No Prisoners

Your department's morale is flagging because your people think it's them versus upper management. Unfortunately, you fall into the management grouping, and you're ready to put them all on probation.

What's Wrong?

 Your team is losing trust in their leadership.

 Productivity is down.

 This kind of "teamwork" can lead to mutiny.

 Perception can be difficult to change.

 You're stuck in the middle.

 Putting them on probation will only make the situation worse.

 You're having nightmares in which you're always one of those assassinated czars.

Some Success Strategies:

Try communicating with "them" to see if their grievances are real. If so, then it's your responsibility to take their case to your management. If the issue is perception, then you must maintain morale from your level by being as fair as possible. Show that you're not on anyone's side, but that you're simply trying to get the job done. You might worry if they begin speaking in Russian.

#36 Power To The People!

The latest trend in management is empowerment and participative management which enables people to work in self-directed work teams. You think such concepts are *stupid* (now where have we seen that word before?) and detract from your role as supervisor.

What's Wrong?

 You don't have faith in your people.

 You're a control freak.

 You're afraid your staff might perform better than with you supervising.

 You're not a progressive thinker.

 You're sure this is the first stage of communism.

Some Success Strategies:

C'mon, give your employees a chance. Begin by giving them minor assignments and see how they're handled. Appoint team leaders. With each success you increase the level of responsibility. It's rewarding to both you and your management when your department is running efficiently without constant supervision.

#37 Daily Turn-Ons

It's getting tougher and tougher to motivate your people. You dangle the usual raises and promotions, but that's no longer working. And, cutbacks have reduced the amount of promotions and bonuses available.

What's Wrong?

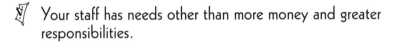

☑ Your staff has needs other than more money and greater responsibilities.

☑ You're not taking the time to find out what their needs are.

☑ Your staff is not communicating with you.

☑ After a job well done, a dollar bill taped to their PC monitor isn't cutting it.

Some Success Strategies:

Find out what your people value. Be as flexible as possible with such issues as family illness, school activities, child care, etc. If possible, schedule flex hours. Take your people off-site occasionally to brainstorm ideas and motivate. Perhaps a weekend getaway will be revitalizing. Be sure your staff, if deserving, shares equally in rewards: career opportunities, assigned parking, plaques, etc. Remember, listen to your people.

#38 Burn, Baby, Burn

Some of your staff have been acting kind of strange lately. They seem apathetic, confused, and depressed. Rumors have it that two are looking for other jobs. Somebody mentioned these symptoms as indicative of burnout, but you're thinking of bringing in a shrink at lunch time.

What's Wrong?

 You're going to suffer a major fallout in your department.

 Your staff has been under great pressure, or, perhaps, they've suffered some disappointment.

 Some of your staff may be undergoing personal strife.

 Your team is suffering burnout.

 That shrink could have everyone realizing they always loved their mothers, but hate their supervisor.

© 1983,1991 CHARLES BARSOTTI

Some Success Strategies:

CBarsotti

Burnout is that sudden loss of motivation, enthusiasm, and interest for a job. You need to identify it immediately and remake the job into something exciting. Offer new challenges and training. Find out from your team members what motivates them. Support and be empathetic. Give clearly defined guidelines to achieve the desired goals. Rejuvenate your staff.

#39 Able To Leap Tall Buildings & An Occasional Short Desk

You hear all the good things about empowerment and it seems to be working well in your department. Except for two of your people, who don't seem to embrace or feel comfortable with the concept.

What's Wrong?

- The duo doesn't see the big picture.

- They're less motivated and will concentrate on vacation, personal "stuff," etc.

- They're nervous about straying from the "tried and true" organizational procedures.

- They're not really part of the "new" empowered team.

- They're no superheroes, and if you don't do something, you're no supervisor.

Some Success Strategies:

Help them to develop the self-confidence necessary to create solutions. To start, give them small projects. Ask for a blueprint on how they'll achieve their goals. See what you get. Offer assistance, but only direction (when asked). Allow them to make mistakes. Praise progress. Ask them for their thoughts during meetings. Get them to realize the powerful role they can play when thinking, executing, and resolving issues on their own.

Chapter 4

Relationships

#40 Great Job, I'll Take The Credit Now

One of your staff made an excellent cost-saving suggestion, which you modified somewhat and for which you then took full credit.

What's Wrong?

⭐ You've been deceitful.

⭐ You've lost the respect of your staff member.

⭐ You've created a breach of trust.

⭐ If upper management finds out, you may be circulating your resume.

⭐ You're better suited for politics.

Some Success Strategies:

Give success to those who deserve it. You'll foster stronger relationships with your people if they can trust you. If you do improve or enhance their initial suggestion, then ask yourself if it's so important that you share credit. The credit may mean much more to that resourceful staff member than it does to you.

#41 Coffee, Tea, Or?

One of your more attractive employees has been making suggestive comments. Now this person is wondering if you'd like to meet after work for a coffee.

What's Wrong?

- You're setting yourself up for embarrassment.

- You'll jeopardize the impartial supervision you should be giving your staff.

- Your integrity will be compromised.

- You may be violating company policy.

- Instead of spending your 401(k) on retirement, you can spend it on lawyers.

Some Success Strategies:

Thank your co-worker for the invitation, but you mention that don't think it's a good idea to mix business with pleasure. You don't want to appear aloof or superior, but you are a supervisor and your responsibilities may sometimes carry outside the office or shop. Be conversant and friendly, but remain professional. If a more personal relationship is in the cards, suggest a transfer to a different department.

#42 Be Like Me

You want your staff to be more aggressive (like you) when dealing with customers. You know it will result in more business.

What's Wrong?

 What works for you doesn't work for everybody.

 Conflict with your staff may result, because you'll smother their uniqueness.

 Some of your customers may only respond to a softer approach, not to a blitzkrieg.

 It's unrealistic to believe in the "Stepford Staff."

Some Success Strategies:

Allow your people to develop their business relationships using their own unique tools, their own unique personalities. If it works, don't fix it. If one of your staff isn't getting the job done, then make adjustments. Inform your staff of the techniques that have worked well for you and allow them to adapt it into their own style. The diversity of your customer base is best handled by the diverse abilities of your own people.

#43 Everything On The Side Except The Bun, Please

You enjoy going out to lunch with your staff. But you're often critical of whatever anyone else orders if it's not similar to your own eating habits.

What's Wrong?

- Your people will be very self-conscious about everything they order.

- Instead of starting off with an appetizer, you could start off with an argument.

- This culinary criticism could affect working conditions back in the office.

- Hey, some people just don't eat burgers and fries.

- You're giving someone a reason to resent you.

- You'll find yourself ordering for one.

Some Success Strategies:

Tolerance should be practiced across the lunch table as much as in the office. Being outside the office is a terrific opportunity to "bond" with your people (maybe even, if desired, take your relationship to a more personal level). Don't condemn the salad bar if it makes your associate feel better. And certainly don't comment on his new pair of large, floppy ears.

#44 Don't Let It Go To Your Head...Or Your Stomach

You've recently become a supervisor, and now that you're in management, you don't feel so bad taking an occasional Friday off, or extending that lunch break an extra half-hour.

What's Wrong?

⧗ You're not setting a good example for your people.

⧗ Your staff will resent you (and envy you, too).

⧗ There's a morale problem.

⧗ Upper management won't be too happy.

⧗ That'll be an extra two hours a week on the stationary bike.

Some Success Strategies:

Understand that your new position is not a license to abuse your privileges. You are expected to be more responsible, not less. You need to offer your people guidance and much of this is done by setting a good example. Take a normal lunch break and be there to help your department. Wake-up! Rank doesn't necessarily have its privileges.

#45 State Of The Union

You work in a union environment and nonassigned jobs are not getting done without arguments. You think it's because the union is against management. You're angry enough to fire everyone.

What's Wrong?

♦ Your department is not meeting deadlines.

♦ You're not making any friends.

♦ You've allowed emotions to cloud the issue; cooperation will be difficult.

♦ You've created even more work for yourself.

♦ You'll never get your own union card.

Some Success Strategies:

Work at developing a relationship with the union employees and shop stewards. They will work with you (more often than not) if you're their ally. Be familiar with the union rules and job descriptions. Understand them and avoid confrontation because of confusion.

#46 Get A Life!

You're completely dedicated to your job. You can't understand why your people get upset when you ask them to stay late for an unscheduled meeting, or come in on that free Saturday. Of course, you don't have any social life, but that shouldn't make any difference.

What's Wrong?

* ✗ Your people <u>do</u> have lives outside of work.

* ✗ You're not creating harmony within your team, only discord.

* ✗ Your life is certainly not balanced.

* ✗ Your reputation will keep away new employee prospects.

* ✗ Unbeknownst to you, your staff places a flattering, but completely untrue ad for you in the local paper's "Singles Personal Section" and now you just want to stay home to answer the phone.

Some Success Strategies:

Be considerate of your people's free time. If a special project needs extra attention, then ask who might like to assist you. If the project demands a particular skill, perhaps some of your staff might appreciate development in this area. If weekend work is necessary, explain why it's important. If you can't explain it, then you probably should check out a video dating service. Consider giving time off in the future in exchange for the extra time now.

#47 Friends Are Friends, But The People I Supervise Are...?

You've recently been promoted to supervisor and some of your friends, now your subordinates, are taking advantage of their relationship with you. You don't know if you should report them to upper management or ignore them.

What's Wrong?

♦ You're being tested in your new role as a supervisor.

♦ You're being tested as a friend.

♦ If you report them, you'll build a wall of animosity.

♦ If you ignore them, the problem may never disappear and others may do the same.

♦ Your Christmas card list just got smaller.

Some Success Strategies:

Confront your employees and discuss the situation. Without being defensive, discuss the situation with them. You don't appreciate it, and neither would upper management (if they found out). You want to work together and make your department as efficient as possible. Act fairly and don't overreact. Seek advice from experienced managers who have had similar circumstances.

#48 Divorce & Remarry

Your mentor, the person who hired you, has been terrific, but now she adds very little to your learning base. You'd like to break it off and find another mentor, but you don't want to hurt her feelings. And you're not sure how to find a new mentor. Maybe place an ad in the organization's newspaper?

What's Wrong?

- You're wasting your time and that of your mentor's.

- You're putting your career on hold.

- Your frustration level will only build.

- Your mentor will sense your unhappiness.

- Maybe your mentor, gentle soul that she is, would like to tell you to "get lost."

© 1993, 1994 AL ROSS

Some Success Strategies:

Tactfully, approach your mentor and thank her for all that she's done for you. Explain how you'd like to move on. She'll understand. If she doesn't, belittle her, but do it graciously. Keep your eyes open for a mentor you not only can trust, but someone with whom you can also, obviously, grow with. Share goals with your prospective mentor to confirm that you're on the same track. Understand what you'd both like to gain from the relationship.

#49 Oh No, More Tips On Fly Fishing

You're quite the amiable guy and love to talk at lunch, after work, etc. with your people. You've always got so much to say, that you usually lead the discussions on subject matters of your choosing.

What's Wrong?

- No one else can ever talk about their interests.

- You won't learn much about your people if you dominate the conversation.

- People may feel ignorant about the subject matter you're talking about.

- People may feel <u>you're</u> ignorant because you don't know about other things.

- You're taking advantage of a captive audience.

- Keep it up and your talks will be monologues.

Some Success Strategies:

Give others a chance to choose the subject matter. Maybe it won't be about last night's ballgame, but perhaps you'll learn something you didn't know. You'll definitely learn more about your staff. Ask questions. Draw the discussion out. Be participative, but not in a dominating manner.

#50 Forget The Fast Track, You're Way Off Track

Lately, you've taken to criticizing your manager. You "bad mouth" him to almost anyone who will listen.

What's Wrong?

- You're setting a bad example.

- You're showing a lack of respect.

- Others may think they can criticize freely also.

- Your boss might find out.

- Your working environment becomes negative and hostile.

- And now, you just heard your boss tell someone that <u>you</u> chew with your mouth open.

"My Boss is such a nerd!"

Some Success Strategies:

Keep any negative feelings about your boss to yourself. If you have to vent, share your frustration with a trusted friend. Share the frustration you're experiencing with your boss. He may not be aware of the tension. If the relationship doesn't improve, pay a visit to your resource manager. If you simply cannot tolerate your manager, find another position. If you don't, your true feelings will eventually be recognized.

Chapter 5

Discipline

#51 Catch It On The 11:00 News

You launch into a harsh and lengthy criticism of one of your people in front of everyone.

What's Wrong?

 You may have made a long-lasting enemy.

 If you don't have all your facts right, you'll be the one with egg on your face.

 You foster dissension in the ranks.

 You've embarrassed this person before his peers.

 Your staff will be afraid to express themselves.

 You'll have to hire someone to taste your food.

Some Success Strategies:

Keep the strong criticism between you and your subordinate in a private setting. Save both of you from a possible major embarrassment. There could also be a logical explanation why something went wrong. This is further reason to meet with just your associate. Take time to uncover all the pertinent information.

#52 Leapfrog

One of your staff isn't pleased with your work assignments, and is taking her complaints to your boss. You just ignore it.

What's Wrong?

 Your authority is being undermined.

 Your boss is getting involved in subject matter that doesn't directly concern her.

 You won't develop any relationship with the critical employee.

 If not stopped, you'll be the subject of a new dance craze, "The Leapfrog," and everybody will be doing it!!

Some Success Strategies:

You need to talk to your management to see how they might respond. Perhaps they'll refer future staff concerns to you. If not, then you'll have to discuss the protocol directly with the "leapfrogging" employee. For you to maintain your credibility, the proper chain of authority must be recognized.

#53 Instead Of Watches, Give Alarm Clocks

Your people are frequently late for work. When reminded about being on time, they do fine for the next week or so, then *whoops*! Car didn't start, traffic was terrible, kids lied about what schools they were being dropped off at, and you'd just like to fire all of them!

What's Wrong?

- Staff is testing your authority.

- You're losing productivity.

- You're losing the ability to direct your team.

- If a few can get away with it, others may follow.

- Since words can never hurt them, it might be time to go for the sticks and stones.

Some Success Strategies:

If meeting with your people and explaining the importance of being on time hasn't worked, then discipline is necessary. Not the rack, perhaps, but have the employee make up the work at the end of the day. Late arrivals can be given unpleasant tasks, or maybe the last one in has to be the rotten egg. You must also document in writing when your people are late, and keep the document in their personal files. Or, deduct the lost time from their paycheck.

#54 Should I Speak Up Or Forever Hold My Peace?

One of your people is having personal problems and it's beginning to affect his performance. You're ready to confront him and tell him to separate personal concerns from business issues, and just do his job.

What's Wrong?

👄 You could just make the matter worse.

👄 You may not understand the seriousness of the personal dilemma.

👄 You'll seem unsympathetic, uncaring, and not very nice.

👄 You're probably not real good material for the Peace Corps.

Some Success Strategies:

See if the problem resolves itself without your intervention. If not, then meet (not confront) and explain your problem. Determine if and how his co-workers are being affected by this problem. See how long this subpar performance has been going on. Also, find out the subject of the problem before addressing the employee. Remember that you're ideally trying to find the balance between maintaining productivity, and expressing your empathy.

#55 Off With Their Heads!

You're getting extremely irritated, because your people are spending too much time making personal calls, exchanging juicy gossip, and setting up office betting pools.

What's Wrong?

 Lax attitude is contagious.

 It could become the norm.

 Your responsibility to positively influence the behavior of the others is in question.

 You're not in on the gossip <u>or</u> the betting pools.

Some Success Strategies:

Be alert. Monitor closely what's going on and let your employees know that you don't appreciate them taking advantage of their positions. Don't condone, but be lenient during special periods, such as holidays. Talk with the people that abuse working hours excessively or frequently. Clearly communicate the company's policy about personal calls and gambling.

#56 Take Him To The Shed

One of your people can't take any suggestions or direction without arguing, and you're not sure how to handle him. He's a good worker, but he's testing your patience.

What's Wrong?

🏠 He's also testing your authority.

🏠 Not wanting to deal with this individual creates a communications gap.

🏠 His behavior negatively impacts teamwork.

🏠 If he gets his way, others may try the same tactic.

🏠 He reminds you of your spouse.

Some Success Strategies:

Promote the issue of teamwork. Try to convince him of his value in doing various tasks. Be prepared for his arguments. Remember, you're the boss and if all else fails, perhaps disciplinary action is the only solution. It's time to call his mother.

#57 Liar, Liar, Integrity's On Fire!

Everyone tells a little white lie now and then, but one of your staff has been lying repeatedly, and, though you'd like to ignore him, you're really not sure what to do.

What's Wrong?

🔥 How will you be able to believe anything he tells you?

🔥 His lies will weaken the integrity of the department.

🔥 Left unchecked, this behavior will reflect poorly on you.

🔥 If he can get away with it, maybe others will try.

🔥 He should quit and go to law school.

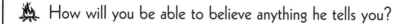

Some Success Strategies:

Research events in question and confirm falsehoods. Confront employee in private, produce verified data, and ask for an explanation. If the employee continues to proclaim his innocence, then document his behavior, and your responses. Also watch carefully to see if his nose grows. If he admits to lying, then you'll have to examine the circumstances, and take appropriate measures.

#58 Ready, Aim, Fire!

One of your people, who has had a bad attitude lately, has now ruined a major project with her carelessness. You're so furious you're going to fire her on the spot.

What's Wrong?

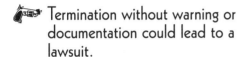
Termination without warning or documentation could lead to a lawsuit.

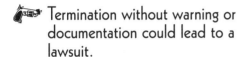
The employee could have some personal problem that's affecting her work.

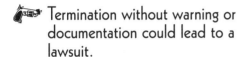
Perhaps you shouldn't have assigned this individual to the project.

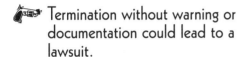
Termination without thought could lead to departmental chaos.

Some Success Strategies:

Sit down with the employee and explain the situation. Ask for her side of the story. If her side is unsatisfactory, warn, and then begin documentation. Note problems with assignments, being tardy, uncooperative, etc. Let the employee know what she has to do to get her act together. If the slide continues, then terminate. And don't let the employee hang around during the two-week notice period. Her presence will likely be detrimental to her co-workers and your productivity. Keep your manager informed of your intervention with this employee and discuss your options.

#59 Has Great People Skills And A Strong Left Jab

Lately, one of your people has been emotional, subject to angry outbursts, and confrontational. You're thinking he will just improve with time.

What's Wrong?

- You could be ignoring a time bomb.

- He's creating very unpleasant working conditions.

- The department will certainly be less productive.

- Someone's feelings have probably already been hurt.

- You think martial arts is some kind of painting for you and your spouse.

Some Success Strategies:

Violence in the workplace usually has a long fuse. Watch for telltale signs of volatility, frustration, confrontations, argumentation, etc. Keep open the communication lines with your people so you can detect any changes. If spotted, have the employee take a little time off. That may defuse the situation. Do not tolerate any violence, and that includes verbal attacks. If things look like they're going to get out of control, don't hesitate to call security.

#60 Off To Work We Go (Or Maybe We're Sick)

A group within your department is very close; and, to make a point, they will sometimes stage a "sick-out" in which the whole group is out for a day or two. They call in sick, or with other acceptable excuses.

What's Wrong?

⚙ You're losing productivity.

⚙ This group has little respect for their jobs and responsibilities.

⚙ They are setting terrible examples for new team members.

⚙ When they're out, you have to scramble to hire temps, fill departmental needs, etc.

⚙ This group is setting a negative precedent for the whole organization.

⚙ Unfortunately, after fighting for teamwork and productivity, you're really coming down with something.

Some Success Strategies:

Communicate with your team on what the policy is for this type of behavior. Make them aware of problems their absence is causing in the department and throughout the organization. Focus on specific or individual problem areas. Try using rewards like time off for excellent attendance. Develop bonus program for departmental improvements. If nothing seems to work, then you should seriously consider staff changes.

#61 Knifing Her Way To The Top

One of the latest additions to your department has the reputation of "backstabbing," or undermining the efforts of others, to achieve her success.

What's Wrong?

🔪 She'll destroy the integrity of the department.

🔪 Your job will be much more difficult.

🔪 Besides sabotaging her co-workers, she could have you targeted.

🔪 You can only approach her in a frontal position.

Some Success Strategies:

Take the weapon out of her hands. Don't act on what she says about others, unless, of course, there is the possibility of truth. Don't ignore her verbal attacks on others. Make it clear that her method of operating will not be condoned.

#62 Meet Me Behind The Water Cooler After Work

One of your staff members is a big man and he uses this to his advantage by bullying his co-workers. He doesn't hit them, but he intimidates with his size, making them take blame for his mistakes or doing him favors. He's a good worker when he wants to be, but you're thinking of transferring him. If not, he might want your office next.

What's Wrong?

🥀 Your people will never work as well when trembling.

🥀 Neither will you.

🥀 You'll have to focus more of your time on the bully and not on your responsibilities.

🥀 His disruptive behavior will not allow you to get a true reading on what everyone else in the department is accomplishing.

🥀 He'll start demanding your lunch money.

Some Success Strategies:

Watch the bully and let him know he's being monitored. Let him know that his behavior is unacceptable. Don't try to bully back. Promise rewards if other routes can be found and positive results can be achieved. Always give praise if these efforts are successful. Conversely, promise corrective disciplinary action if his poor behavior persists.

Chapter 6

Recognition

#63 An 8.5—Easy To Dance To

In rating your people for their performance appraisals, you always rate them against the top employee.

What's Wrong?

 It is unfair, because the top person may have been doing the job the longest.

 It is unfair, because job responsibilities could be different.

 The top employee may be thought of as the "supervisor's pet," and it'll be discouraging for others to try to compete.

 It will create resentment toward the top person (just like in Social Studies when someone ruined the curve by knowing <u>all</u> the state capitals).

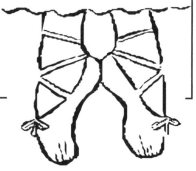

Some Success Strategies:

Develop a set of objective guidelines that everyone will be measured against. Develop individual performance plans based on the position of the person and his correct set of skills and competencies. Be thoroughly prepared. Keep notes on each individual throughout the year to help jog the memory on successes and failures. Give yourself time to think about what each employee has done and what he set out to do.

#64 She Always Liked Him Best

Another supervisor in your department got a bigger raise than you did and you don't understand why. You're going to confront your boss and find out.

What's Wrong?

- 💰 You don't know all the facts.

- 💰 You could create a rift between you and your boss.

- 💰 You could create interdepartmental tension.

- 💰 It probably wasn't a good idea at your boss's last birthday party to tell her she looks great, and then ask if that's her original face.

Some Success Strategies:

Relax. Maybe your co-worker was hired at a lower pay scale than you and has just been elevated to equal status. Maybe she deserved more of a raise. There is probably a legitimate reason for her raise being greater than yours. See what you can do to warrant the same kind of increase. Perhaps she also displays more tact. Try playing the game.

#65 When The Team Flower Is A Forget-Me-Not

You only recognize the top performer in your department and tend to ignore the solid, but unspectacular ones. This same person also takes his vacation in Hawaii every year.

What's Wrong?

❀ Your staffers may cry favoritism.

❀ Your solid performers may be doing their best.

❀ You'll create resentment between #1 and the rest of the staff.

❀ You'll erode the self-esteem of everyone else in the department.

❀ Your staff could get suspicious when you always return from vacation at the same time as #1...with a tan.

Some Success Strategies:

Recognize everyone in some way. Give awards or incentives according to the performance capabilities of the individual. You can't expect the same performance from a new employee as you would from an experienced one. Contribution and a sense of value are very important to establishing self-esteem and teamwork. Besides rewards, frequent praise and encouragement are recommended.

#66 When I Blow My Horn, Why Does Everyone Cover Their Ears?

You'd like to gain some recognition for your achievements, but you don't seem to be getting anywhere. Upper management doesn't recognize your contributions even though production is up and your staff seems very satisfied.

What's Wrong?

♪ You haven't learned how to play the game yet.

♪ Maybe you're expecting too much.

♪ You need to support yourself with good people that can also *sing* your praises.

♪ You're not communicating your performance to upper-management clearly.

♪ Perhaps management is tone-deaf.

Some Success Strategies:

Volunteer for a project that is high-profile. Get on a committee network internally. See if the boss needs your assistance. Become an expert in some discipline. If all else fails, surround yourself with a full orchestra.

#67 Color Me Green

Your idea of recognition is money. Everyone should be appreciative of pay raises, commissions, and the occasional bonus.

What's Wrong?

♦ People are motivated by different things.

♦ You've probably never seen any recognition other than money either. Even as a kid.

♦ You don't realize some forms of recognition last far longer than money.

♦ More money doesn't instill teamwork.

♦ You're losing it when your idea of a good time is hanging out at the local ATM.

Some Success Strategies:

Find out what motivates your team members. Some employees want more than a paycheck. A gift certificate offers a personal touch. Public recognition, dinner on the town, or even a chocolate-covered croissant can be very rewarding. Well, it helps if you like chocolate. Appreciation can also be found in a plaque of achievement that'll hang on the wall, reminding the employee of the superior job she did. Be creative.

#68 Appraisals Are Like Anniversaries

You've just received your third notice from personnel demanding an appraisal for one of your staff. You kept forgetting, now you're late, and you're rushing to get it done by the end of the day. But you can't even remember what your employee was doing back in the first part of the year.

What's Wrong?

▤ You obviously haven't kept accurate records.

▤ You're not fulfilling your duties as a supervisor.

▤ You could get into trouble with your management.

▤ Any appraisal you do now will be incomplete.

▤ You probably can't remember your anniversary either.

Some Success Strategies:

Keep accurate records throughout the year. Note the performance of the employee during the year, not only at the end of it. Conduct informal evaluations throughout the year. Invest time and thought into your appraisals. Give consideration to what your qualified employee may be striving for next. See if you're wearing a wedding band.

#69 I'll Take The Kid With His Glove On The Wrong Hand

Ten people in your department are competing for just one promotion. You've decided to pick the one person who had the lowest performance review only because you want to get rid of him.

What's Wrong?

- You'll hurt the company.

- You'll damage your reputation.

- You're incapable of managing underperformers.

- You're unable to develop the necessary skills and knowledge your people need to do their jobs effectively.

- You'll send a negative message to the rest of your staff.

- What if this is how you got promoted?

Some Success Strategies:

Make your selection fairly with clearly articulated guidelines. Be sure your employees understand exactly what the promotion requires to minimize disappointment. Let those who are disappointed know why they didn't get the promotion. You don't want resentment surrounding you. Focus on the assets they'll continue to add to the department.

#70 Flattery Behind Closed Doors

You feel it's important to praise your staff, but you only do it in private.

What's Wrong?

💙 Makes praise seem less meaningful because it's in private.

💙 Wastes potent impact of "moment" when done in private.

💙 Employee misses "double shot" of congratulations from co-workers.

💙 You're missing opportunity for team to see rewards of job well done (i.e., public praise).

💙 Well, it's still okay to praise your dog in private, he won't care.

Some Success Strategies:

Praise freely, but with sincerity. Praise with specifics, not just with "job well done." Praise often. As noted, keep it out of the closet. Praise toward the goals you want your team to achieve.

#71 U.S.D.A. Approved

Your staff doesn't seem to appreciate the true value of quality. Your attitude isn't much different. You think you can still put out a good product without being so quality-conscious.

What's Wrong?

- Your diminishment in quality is inconsistent with the goals of the organization.

- Customers will notice lower quality levels.

- You'll lose business.

- Your management will recognize this laxness, and you'll pay the penalty.

- Good people are motivated and sustained by doing quality work.

- You don't mind driving a Yugo.

Some Success Strategies:

Quality should be a top priority. Establish a quality team to review what your work group must do to better serve the customer. Set quality standards. Adopt a continuous improvement attitude toward quality. Reward those who make the extra effort to develop and maintain quality.

#72 I Don't Love You, But Would You Stay With Me Forever?

One of your best employees is looking for advancement in other areas. You can't stand the thought of losing her, and hesitate to give her any direction or assistance.

What's Wrong?

- You're limiting this person's chance for growth.

- This person will resent you and her future performance may reflect this.

- Others will feel that you're not there to help them improve and advance.

- Less qualified employees may fill these advanced positions.

- You're punishing people for doing too good of a job.

- You're selfish.

- You're overdoing this "bonding" thing.

Some Success Strategies:

Be prepared to assist your better employees in moving forward. Have someone else in the wings, or in training when you see that position being vacated. Always encourage advancement. You're more likely to get better applicants when they realize the support they'll receive.

Chapter 7

Change

#73 Where's A Shredder When I Need One?

You find yourself buried in paperwork; and, aside from having trouble breathing, you're leaving the office later and later, and getting more and more frustrated.

What's Wrong?

 You won't be doing a good a job if overworked.

Your health could suffer.

If you have a family, you could become a stranger.

You're probably collecting a lot of worthless paper and fail to recognize it.

You're a supervisor, not a pencil pusher.

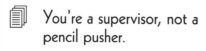 You're starting to throw lit matches at your In-basket.

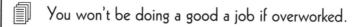

Some Success Strategies:

Try to sort your paperwork every day and put it in stacks. Not random stacks, but with action tags attached, such as: priority; non-priority with less immediate action; read and forward; read and keep; and great for origami. Now you can handle your workload with emphasis on priority issues. Skim the less relevant material or retain until later.

#74 Where's My Life Preserver?

Your organization is downsizing and some people have already been laid-off. Your staff is very concerned about their positions, but you decide it's best to tell them nothing.

What's Wrong?

✗ Morale will be terrible.

✗ Paranoia will be rampant.

✗ The gossip mill will be the only thing working full-time.

✗ Upper management will not admire your leadership skills.

✗ Teamwork will only be found in group therapy.

Some Success Strategies:

Communicate with your people and try to keep them informed. Have meetings whenever you deem them necessary. Handle your responsibilities with confidence and do business as usual. Instill this same confidence in your staff. Stop rumors before they get out of control.

#75 Hard To Say No

You've just taken over a new department. You have absolutely no idea if all these challenging assignments your staff is being given can be completed successfully, or on time. You don't know what to tell management.

What's Wrong?

➤ You don't know the capabilities of your staff.

➤ The restroom is around the corner, but so is chaos.

➤ You have no specific goals, only those of completing the given tasks.

➤ You'd like to quit, but you're so confused you forgot how to do it.

Some Success Strategies:

Evaluate the work progressing through your area. Identify the steps it goes through and the processes involved. Know the capabilities of each of your staff. Estimate the time involved for each task. Look for better ways to do the job. If you know just what your department can do, then you'll never be guilty of trying to do too much, and not doing it successfully.

#76 How Job Descriptions Can Be Like Dodo Birds

Your staff has taken on new challenges over the last few years, and you now realize those original job descriptions for which you hired and evaluated upon might as well be extinct. They're worthless.

What's Wrong?

📄 You can't hire someone new without knowing what specific skills you're looking for.

📄 You can't evaluate your people with a blueprint that's outdated.

📄 Some might rebel against doing anything that isn't part of their original job description.

📄 You can't take on new responsibilities without knowing what your people are doing.

📄 Evaluating your team members will become increasingly difficult.

📄 It'll be so embarrassing when management can only determine the origins of your earlier job descriptions by carbon dating.

Some Success Strategies:

Update your job descriptions. Ask people in each job position to document what they do. Benchmark and note activities of successful people. List skills and knowledge necessary for each job activity. Check list for accuracy. Add narrative of what each staff person does. Include intangibles that are part of every job, and also the job's daily chronology.

#77 Perms Instead Of Temps

You have no desire to work with temporary employees; you prefer the permanent kind.

What's Wrong?

✧ You could be missing an opportunity to cut administrative overhead.

✧ You are missing an opportunity to create a pool of skilled workers.

✧ You are missing an opportunity to create flexible work schedules.

✧ You are missing an opportunity to "test" the employee before hiring.

✧ Maybe you'll become temporarily unemployed.

PERSONNEL

Some Success Strategies:

Try it. You might like it. Find the right candidate yourself and have the temp agency hire him. Then have the new hire sent to your organization. Educate and observe during the probationary period. Then hire full-time, or release him. If hiring on seasonal or a "true" temporary basis, be sure your temporary workers have the appropriate skills required for the position.

#78 When Downsizing Isn't Going From Size 8 To Size 6

Your organization is downsizing and many of your remaining team members seem affected by it. You just let them agonize over it because you think they will revert to their old ways over time.

What's Wrong?

✗ Lack of motivation because of a "it's probably going to happen to me" attitude.

✗ Diminished morale in department.

✗ Overall pessimism in department.

✗ Apathy toward job and increased absenteeism and tardiness.

✗ Teams members are angry.

✗ Decrease in productivity with team.

✗ You're acting like downsizing is just another "diet fad."

Some Success Strategies:

Address this attitudinal change immediately. Encourage staff to take on new responsibilities. Talk out concerns with your people. Offer emotional support. Establish clear cut assignments and make them exciting. Offer new training, new challenges, and incentives. Tolerate mistakes during this transition. Ensure that everyone is contributing to the bottom line. Rediscover that missing spirit.

#79 Family Size To Byte Size

In an effort to control costs and satisfy work/life balance issues, your company reorganized. As a result, your department has become decentralized and some of your people are working out of their homes. Now you're not having any success in delivering projects on time.

What's Wrong?

- You can't function without having an actual body nearby.

- Your people don't know their own deadlines.

- Information is not being shared.

- Your staff doesn't understand how their role is an integral part of the project.

- You haven't mastered the true communicative value of E-mail, faxes, telephones, etc.

- One of your people sold his house and wants to work out of a Winnebago.

Some Success Strategies:

You need to change the way you manage your people. Keep a log of what you expect and when. Have occasional meetings, but be very well prepared. Be certain your people have access to information that will assist them, utilizing Internet, voice mail, conference calls, etc. Don't leave them isolated. Schedule regular updates to verify work progress.

#80 When PC Doesn't Mean Politically Correct

The computer age is upon you and you're resisting it. Your people are talking some nonsense about e-mail, voice mail, servers, and local area networks. Hey, the computers help out with some things, but they're not the only answer. You have paper files and can still work magic with a legal pad and #2 pencil.

What's Wrong?

- 🖫 You're working in the Dark Ages.

- 🖫 You're becoming less efficient and productive than you could be.

- 🖫 You won't be speaking the same language as everyone around you.

- 🖫 Your staff will lose respect for you.

- 🖫 Competition will charge past you.

- 🖫 You might want to practice writing your resume with a quill.

Some Success Strategies:

Take a class and learn the computer basics. You need to learn not only how to work a computer but how to get the computer to work for you. Work and learn from your computer-literate staff people. Try e-mail and see if it increases your productivity. Open up and be part of the information age.

#81 Do You Have Ten Ones For A Five?

Change is not always good. You're constantly making "enhancements" and suggesting other ways that jobs can be done. Not bad, except this is after your employees thought they had successfully completed their projects.

What's Wrong?

💰 People don't have a chance to provide input before the change.

💰 It's difficult for people to buy into unexpected change.

💰 People will be confused.

💰 Most people resist change.

💰 If your people liked you before, then be prepared for a change.

Some Success Strategies:

Review planned changes with people before they're implemented. Be flexible in adopting the input you receive from people whenever possible. Let people know why these changes are necessary and what impact the changes have on them. Monitor the progress and acceptance of the changes.   Keep yourself tuned into the concerns of the team.

Chapter 8

Training & Team Work

#82 If He Won't Train And Only Complains

You always have your top person train the new hires and all he does is complain. But you're reluctant to change because you want your very best staff members teaching!

What's Wrong?

♦ Your best staff member is training and not doing what he does best—producing!

♦ Your best staff member may not have the patience nor the communication skills suitable for training.

♦ You may be creating a serious rift between you and this person.

♦ The new hire may be overwhelmed by watching the best.

♦ The new hire may try to keep pace with your best and make mistakes in his haste.

♦ Your best staff member has developed an insufferable ego.

Some Success Strategies:

Some top producers don't make the best teachers. Have someone in the department who enjoys and is competent in training do the job. Rotate the role of "peer training." Let your best just be productive and sign autographs.

#83 Does Anyone Have Any Stupid Questions?

One of your new people seemed to catch on pretty quickly; he asked no questions, simply nodded, and leapt into the job. The problem is he's making stupid mistakes, which he could have avoided with a few questions during training.

What's Wrong?

❓ His mistakes are holding back your productivity.

❓ He probably didn't want to seem stupid by asking questions.

❓ Maybe your training is confusing.

❓ Maybe he really is stupid.

Some Success Strategies:

Go back over your training to be sure it's clear and leaves no room for misinterpretation. You can also ask questions to confirm the message is being received and check for understanding. Also check to see if someone else in the department or organization might be responsible for impeding his work efficiency. Remember, there really is no such thing as truly stupid questions. Well, there is, but those are left to the media.

#84 Heads I'm Right, Tails You're Wrong

You're always right. Your staff can make suggestions and you'll listen, but hey, you haven't been wrong since 1975.

What's Wrong?

☞ You're stifling the collective voice of your staff and losing great input.

☞ You're building a wall of resentment.

☞ You're insecure.

☞ You don't realize being wrong can be a learning opportunity.

☞ You're arrogant, close-minded, and probably not a lot of fun at lunch.

Some Success Strategies:

Lighten up. Your staff deals with particular issues that they probably understand far better than you. Listen carefully and open up your mind. Actively pursue their input. This will also help develop teamwork.

#85 Rah! Rah! Okay, Who Forgot The Pom-Poms?

You'd really like to see more team spirit within your department, but everyone seems to be out for themselves.

What's Wrong?

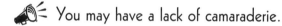 You may have a lack of camaraderie.

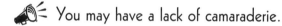 Selfishness will hinder what a team can accomplish.

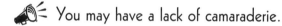 There will be no common goals, only individual goals.

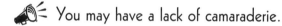 Fighting, egos, and jealousy could severely impact your department.

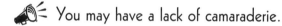 You'll never get a chance to shout SIS BOOM BAH!

Some Success Strategies:

Instill a sense of teamwork in everyone. If not, you may want to get different players. Not everyone is capable of being a productive team player. However, many certainly are willing and able. Create a supportive environment for the team with such simple things as collaborative work methods. Challenge your team and encourage them to use their initiative. Select a team member of the week. Pursue a spirit-enhancing activity. Develop a team slogan.

#86 Don't Talk To Me, I'm A Xenophobe!

Your staff is very diverse, both in culture and background, and you're finding it difficult to fuse these differences into one effective team. So you choose to ignore this diversity and do the best you can.

What's Wrong?

 You're missing the opportunity to recognize and utilize each staff member's strength.

 Not talking to strangers is fine if you're a kid, but you need to communicate.

 You're leaving yourself open to misunderstandings.

 Other staff members may follow your lead.

Some Success Strategies:

Have a little self-awareness training during your regular meetings in which everyone shares information about their experiences, assumptions, etc. Perhaps people will see themselves in the talks of others. Work at developing a sensitivity to your diverse co-workers. Set an example for the rest of your department. Don't be judgmental.

#87 When I Is More Than Just A Pronoun

One of your people prefers to work by himself. He doesn't think he needs anyone else and can do the job much better on his own.

What's Wrong?

 He's certainly not a team player.

 He'll create divisiveness in the department.

 His ego is getting in the way of his own success.

 This "superstar" will not benefit from the collective expertise of his teammates.

 He'll probably start wearing tights and a cape to work.

Some Success Strategies:

Show him the successes the team has achieved and ask if he could have done the same on his own. Then pair him with someone who makes an ideal partner. Give the two of them a project that requires collaboration. Show him the value of teamwork.

#88 You'll Both Go To Bed Without Supper

Two of your staff are constantly bickering, arguing, and fighting. You keep thinking they'll grow up and learn to work with one another.

What's Wrong?

 Their actions are disruptive to the department.

 They're too busy fighting to get as much work done as they could.

 You'll have others on the team taking sides, causing more headaches.

 You're not offering guidance or leadership.

 You heard the combatants say something about loaded pistols at dawn.

Some Success Strategies:

Try bringing the conflicting parties together and attempt to "talk out" the disagreement. Encourage compromise. Be fair and communicate freely. Suggest solutions. Listen to their arguments, and if a supervisor's decision is required, then make it. If all else fails, ask them what their mothers would think.

#89 Mission Possible

You're the team leader. Now, you're developing the team's mission. You don't think you need their input for this.

What's Wrong?

 Your people won't feel any ownership.

 The mission you develop may not be the best for the team.

 It may not provide any guidance or direction for the team.

 The mission may be obsolete before it's even complete.

 Your mission "possible" is quickly becoming "impossible."

Some Success Strategies:

Give everyone the opportunity to participate in creating the mission for the team. Review the existing mission and update it where necessary. Keep it flexible. This is all part of building an effective team. By including your team members in creating the team mission, they will more likely buy into your purpose.

#90 Visual Impact Doesn't Mean Tattoos

You're not a big supporter of visual aids. The charts, goal boards, etc. seem like cheap props to you. You're still a firm believer in hands-on management without the day-glo frills.

What's Wrong?

 You don't have any colorful reminders of team goals.

 You don't think visual reminders have an impact on some people.

 You don't realize that goal tracking is a key element toward goal achievement.

 People may not realize their role as well unless it's posted as part of a chart matrix.

 You probably never laughed at the rubber-nosed circus clown either.

Some Success Strategies:

Add some visual color to the department. Adopt aids that reflect productivity levels, teamwork, and goals. Make them user-friendly (e.g., don't complicate with too many icons, text, etc.). Post them in an appropriate location.

Chapter 9

Meetings &
Other Stupid Stuff

#91 Out Of The Loop

As a supervisor you're not holding regular meetings with the group, or meeting one-to-one. Your staff contends you have no idea what's going on.

What's Wrong?

○ You seem uninterested in the business.

○ Your value as a resource will be minimized since you're out of touch.

○ Expect a communication jam when upper management demands departmental updates, and all you provide are attendance records.

○ Staff thinks you don't appreciate their value.

○ An unscrupulous staff person could take advantage of your seemingly apathetic attitude.

○ Your staff will begin to wonder why you're here at all and you'll become a philosophical debate: Is there a supervisor? And how do we know?

Some Success Strategies:

Hold regular meetings if ongoing issues need to be cross-examined and discussed. If schedules and job demands don't require group meetings, then it's important you know what your staff is doing. It's equally important they know that you know. They'll be more comfortable in sharing their activities and, if inclined, far less likely to be deceptive. You'll be part of the team.

#92 Now, If I Was Only Paid By The Meeting

You find meetings a valuable forum for exchanging ideas and, to the growing displeasure of your staff, you schedule them frequently. They find too many meetings a waste of productive time.

What's Wrong?

🕐 Maybe they <u>are</u> a waste of time.

🕐 Unhappy associates will not make for productive meetings.

🕐 Eventually all meetings, even the truly important ones, will be approached with resentment.

🕐 Some of your staff may not actually participate in a meeting environment.

🕐 Think of the labor costs sitting in that meeting room; it better be productive.

🕐 Perhaps you just don't like to be left alone.

Some Success Strategies:

Get input from your staff on what subject matter would be most useful for a meeting. Plan an agenda and stick to it. Also, ask yourself what subjects could be better handled without getting together. Ask for questions that can be answered during the meeting. After any meeting, determine if your goals were met. Be cognizant of who contributed to the discussion. If a staff member seems resistant to contribute, find out why. Perhaps speaking in front of her peers makes her uncomfortable. Summarize meeting minutes and distribute them to appropriate persons.

#93 Wait A Minute, I Haven't Even Read The Paper Yet

You're notorious for scheduling meetings first thing in the morning when you're upbeat and roaring to start the day. You're hated for it.

What's Wrong?

- Your staff may be inattentive and ill-tempered at this hour.

- Your staff will fall asleep.

- Your staff may quit.

- This meeting time is simply not productive if you're the only one involved.

- Your people may be tardy for meetings first thing in the morning.

- Your exuberance at this hour may lead your staff to think different creative thoughts, like "101 Painful Ways I Can Wipe That Stupid Grin off My Supervisor's Face."

Some Success Strategies:

Be reasonable and flexible. If the majority of your staff is nocturnal, perhaps you should schedule a meeting time that is favorable for everyone. You may try to alternate between morning and afternoon meetings. Don't always dictate to your internal clock and think the early bird catches the worm. Some people actually prefer a double latte and muffin.

#94 The Mouth That Roared

During meetings and presentations you have a tendency to dominate the discussion, and sometimes you just ramble on.

What's Wrong?

 You sound foolish, and lose credibility.

 You may say something you'll regret.

 You're forgetting to listen.

 This isn't putting you on the fast track into management.

 You're better suited to be a radio talk show host.

Some Success Strategies:

Listen more. If you're giving a presentation, practice keeping it concise. Time yourself. Know exactly how much you have to say. Be aware of your audience; if they're snoring, perhaps you'll want to change course. Formulate your thoughts before you talk.

#95 Wait 'Till You Hear This One

You love to tell jokes, but besides not being very funny, they're sometimes inappropriate.

What's Wrong?

 You're offensive and insulting.

 You could be leaving yourself open for a harassment suit.

 You won't like management's punchline.

 Your image is forever tarnished.

 Your next career step is a sleazy lounge in Las Vegas.

Some Success Strategies:

Clean up your act. You shouldn't jeopardize your position or the reputation of your organization with such juvenile behavior. It's okay to try out some funny material, but remember you're a professional. It may sound trite, but treat the people around you with respect and you can expect the same in return.

#96 And Could You Pick Up My Tie At The Cleaners?

You've given one of your staff a laundry list of things to do; in fact, one of the requests is to pick up your clothes at the dry cleaners.

What's Wrong?

🔸 Unless specially stated beforehand, your staff member wasn't hired to run your personal errands.

🔸 It's disrespectful behavior.

🔸 Apparently, you show very little regard for this staff person's interoffice skills.

🔸 Personal errands should not be subsidized by your organization.

🔸 Imagine how your reputation will suffer if you don't tip well.

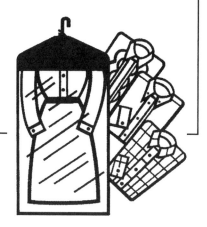

Some Success Strategies:

You're part of a business and during business hours, that's what should be conducted. If you're having difficulty taking care of your personal business, then perhaps, you'll have to make time at lunch. And the emphasis is on YOU, and your responsibilities. You wouldn't want to be picking up a mushroom pizza for your supervisor, would you?

#97 Watch Out
For The "Isms"!

A few of your opinionated and outspoken staff people are arguing about a woman's place in the workplace. Still another chimes in with his thoughts on older people not being committed to long-term results; they're more interested in retirement. You think it's best to ignore them all.

What's Wrong?

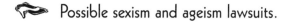 Possible sexism and ageism lawsuits.

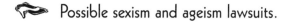 You sticking your head in the ground may lead to further divisive commentary.

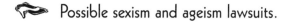 Your authority and control is undermined.

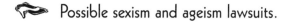 Offended staffers may quit.

 How will you feel about hiring a qualified older woman now?

Some Success Strategies:

Make sure everyone understands the company's policies. Make it clear what cannot be discussed within the department and organization. Create a set of rules and regulations preventing anyone from participating in dialogue that may be perceived as insensitive. Forbid proselytizing. That has nothing to do with artificial limbs, but while we're at it, don't make cracks about them either.

#98 He Sure Looked Good On Paper

The last three people you've hired for your department have quit or been terminated. Yet their references were impeccable and their resumes outstanding.

What's Wrong?

📄 Maybe they were "stretching the truth" on their resumes.

📄 You didn't ask the right questions during interviews.

📄 You were easily "sold" on personality and a slick resume.

📄 You're a rotten judge of character.

📄 A bell should go off when your applicant and his references have the same last name.

Some Success Strategies:

Ask detailed questions during the interview process. Open up the interview so the ensuing dialogue reveals the applicant's personality. Look for motivation. Carefully check references. Look for the characteristics in the individual that are required for the job. You also hire on your "gut" feel, but remember to look for aptitude. Ask yourself how this person would fit in with your team. Enlist the help of other supervisors in your organization or the human resources department in helping you interview and select the right person.

#99 Where Are The Lifeguards?

It's casual dress day, but two of your team members are dressed a little too casual. Their clothes look more like bathing suits than casual business attire.

What's Wrong?

- Department loses sense of professionalism.

- Others may follow this example.

- Performance standards may be relaxed along with dress code.

- Everyone will be calling for the surf report.

Some Success Strategies:

Establish standards that compromise between this beachwear and formal business wear. Have everyone understand what "casual" really means. Refer to the company's dress code or policy. Be specific as to what cannot be worn: cut-offs, bathing suits, sandals, polyester pants, etc. Be sure everyone wears sunblock.

#100 A Mistake Shouldn't Be Like A Life Sentence

When one of your staff makes a mistake, you can't seem to forget it. Oh, they might follow with successes, but you just can't erase that failure. And your people certainly don't appreciate your selective memory.

What's Wrong?

 Your people will lose their confidence.

 They'll be suppressed and afraid to try anything new.

 They'll be labeled as poor performers.

 Your whole department will have a pervasive, negative atmosphere.

 Your reputation as a fair supervisor will certainly be one *forgotten* memory.

Some Success Strategies:

Look at the whole package. Evaluate performance based on agreed upon goals and objectives. Judge the employee on what he's done over the long term, not on one mistake. Accept mistakes as part of the learning process. Give positive reinforcement when appropriate to inspire teamwork and camaraderie.

#101 Intelligent, Efficient, And Extremely Nosy

You feel that the workplace should have no secrets. When your people are gone, you like to wander around their work stations and see what's on their desks. See if any notes have been scribbled on the latest project, who's been stuck on their bulletin board, or what's the latest on their calendars.

What's Wrong?

- Your people will resent their privacy being invaded.

- When people find out you're a snoop, anything you might want to see will be hidden.

- You might not like want you find.

- Your reputation will be damaged.

- Would you like someone going through your desk?

- Curiosity killed the cat. What might it do to the supervisor?

Some Success Strategies:

Just keep your nose to yourself. If you want to see something that pertains to an assignment, ask the person working on it to provide it. If one of your people wants to share something personal from their work space, that's <u>their</u> prerogative. If you need something from that person and he's not around, check only common visable area, such as his in-out basket.

Summary

Think and communicate. If you can remember to do this, you won't find yourself in the land of *stupid* as often.

Take a good, hard look at how you conduct yourself. See if there's room for improvement. See if you've done any of the *stupid* things in this book. And don't be embarrassed if you have. If you haven't, then you're probably not trying.

Focus on the success strategies. You'll surely find some tip that can make you a better supervisor. And a better person.

Good Luck!

About The Publisher

Richard Chang Associates, Inc. is a diversified organizational improvement consulting firm based in Irvine, California. They provide a wide range of products and services to organizations worldwide in the areas of organizational development, quality improvement, team performance, and learning systems. The Publications Division of Richard Chang Associates, Inc., established to provide individuals with a wide variety of practical resources for continuous learning in the workplace or on a personal level, is pleased to bring you this book.

Richard Chang Associates, Inc.
Publications Division
15265 Alton Parkway, Suite 300
Irvine, CA 92618
(800) 756-8096 Fax (714) 727-7007
(714) 727-7477

ADDITIONAL RESOURCES
FROM RICHARD CHANG ASSOCIATES, INC.
PUBLICATIONS DIVISION

Available through Richard Chang Associates, Inc. and training and organizational development resource catalogs worldwide.

PRACTICAL GUIDEBOOK COLLECTION

QUALITY IMPROVEMENT SERIES

Continuous Process Improvement

Continuous Improvement Tools Volume 1

Continuous Improvement Tools Volume 2

Step-By-Step Problem Solving

Meetings That Work!

Improving Through Benchmarking

Succeeding As A Self-Managed Team

Satisfying Internal Customers First!

Process Reengineering In Action

Measuring Organizational Improvement Impact

MANAGEMENT SKILLS SERIES

Coaching Through Effective Feedback

Expanding Leadership Impact

Mastering Change Management

On-The-Job Orientation And Training

Re-Creating Teams During Transitions

Planning Successful Employee Performance

Coaching For Peak Employee Performance

Evaluating Employee Performance

Interviewing And Selecting High Performers

HIGH-IMPACT TRAINING SERIES

Creating High-Impact Training

Identifying Targeted Training Needs

Mapping A Winning Training Approach

Producing High-Impact Learning Tools

Applying Successful Training Techniques

Measuring The Impact Of Training

Make Your Training Results Last

WORKPLACE DIVERSITY SERIES

Capitalizing On Workplace Diversity

Successful Staffing In A Diverse Workplace

Team Building For Diverse Work Groups

Communicating In A Diverse Workplace

Tools For Valuing Diversity

HIGH PERFORMANCE TEAM SERIES

Success Through Teamwork

Building A Dynamic Team

Measuring Team Performance

Team Decision-Making Techniques

Guidebooks are also available in fine bookstores.

ADDITIONAL RESOURCES
FROM RICHARD CHANG ASSOCIATES, INC.
PUBLICATIONS DIVISION

PERSONAL GROWTH AND DEVELOPMENT COLLECTION

Managing Your Career in a Changing Workplace

Unlocking Your Career Potential

Marketing Yourself and Your Career

Making Career Transitions

TRAINING PRODUCTS

Step-By-Step Problem Solving ToolKIT™

Meetings That Work! Practical Guidebook ToolPAK™

Continuous Improvement Tools Volume 1 Practical Guidebook ToolPAK™

101 Stupid Things Trainers Do To Sabotage Success

VIDEOTAPES

Mastering Change Management**

Quality: You Don't Have To Be Sick To Get Better*

Achieving Results Through Quality Improvement*

Total Quality: Myths, Methods, Or Miracles**
  Featuring Drs. Ken Blanchard and Richard Chang

Empowering The Quality Effort**
  Featuring Drs. Ken Blanchard and Richard Chang

TOTAL QUALITY VIDEO SERIES AND WORKBOOKS

Building Commitment**

Teaming Up**

Applied Problem Solving**

Self-Directed Evaluation**

* Produced by American Media Inc.   ** Produced by Double Vision Studios